THE LITTLE BOOK OF
LIVERPOOL

Independent and Unofficial

SEVENTH EDITION

EDITED BY
GEOFF TIBBALS

First published by Carlton Books in 2002
Updated editions 2010, 2013, 2014, 2017, 2019

This edition published in 2021 by OH!
part of Welbeck Publishing Group
20 Mortimer Street, London, W1T 3JW

A CIP catalogue record of this book is available from the British Library.

ISBN 978 1 91161 037 3

Printed in Dubai

10 9 8 7 6 5 4 3 2 1

CONTENTS

INTRODUCTION

Bill Shankly, Tommy Smith, the Kop – the history of
Liverpool Football Club is rich in colourful characters
who have never been short of a sharp one-liner. You
only have to look at the number of ex-Liverpool players
who have become TV pundits. To think, Alan Hansen
was criticised by his former manager for not having
enough to say for himself!

Alongside the shafts of Scouse and Scottish wit, this
book contains more serious quotes offering rare
insights into the private lives and careers of the
players and management staff who have graced
Anfield. So if you want to know what it means to join
Liverpool, to win European trophies, to play under
Jürgen Klopp, or what Paul Ince rates as
better than sex, read on.

CHAPTER 1

THE
LIVERPOOL
WAY

" When you have a Liverpool shirt on your back as part of the squad, you will do anything to make sure you preserve what it stands for. **"**

GERARD HOULLIER

"From my first day at Melwood, I appreciated Liverpool's special DNA."

JOHN BARNES

❝This record sums up our spirit on the field. No player in my team struggles or battles alone. There's always someone there to help him.**❞**

BILL SHANKLY

discussing 'You'll Never Walk Alone'

❝Mind, I've been here during the bad times too. One year we came second.**❞**

BOB PAISLEY

❝Liverpool Football Club is all about winning things and being a source of pride to our fans. It has no other purpose.**❞**

DAVID MOORES

Honorary Life President of Liverpool Football Club

❝This club is the mix of atmosphere, emotion, desire and football quality. Cut off one and it doesn't work. **❞**

JÜRGEN KLOPP

❝The people who come to watch
us play, who love the team and regard it as
part of their lives, would never appreciate
Liverpool having a huge balance in the bank.
They want every asset we possess to be
wearing a red shirt. **❞**

KENNY DALGLISH

ffIt's there to remind our lads
who they're playing for, and to remind the
opposition who they're playing against. **JJ**

BILL SHANKLY

explaining the significance of the 'This Is Anfield' plaque

❝Liverpool had dug its claws ever deeper into our psyche until, at all times, the craving to be simply the best lay just below the surface. **❞**

ALAN EDGE

Faith of our Fathers

"You get to wish that they would just occasionally pass the ball to the other team, like the rest of us do.**"**

Watford boss **GRAHAM TAYLOR**

despairing of playing Liverpool

66 Anfield without European football is like a banquet without wine. **99**

ROY EVANS

❝What attracts you to this club is its history. If you are clever and bright enough, you will look into the history.**❞**

BRENDAN RODGERS

❝It's a magical, magical feeling to walk on to this pitch and think that we are the new owners.**❞**

JOHN W. HENRY

stepping out at Anfield

"If I have to describe this club then it's a big heart and tonight it was pounding like crazy. You could hear it all over the world.**"**

JÜRGEN KLOPP

on the atmosphere at Anfield during their semi-final
second leg victory over Barcelona in the 2019 Champions League

CHAPTER 2

SHANKLY'S SAYINGS

"There are two great teams in Liverpool: Liverpool and Liverpool Reserves. **"**

BILL SHANKLY

"If Everton were playing at the bottom of my garden, I'd draw the curtains.**"**

BILL SHANKLY

"Don't worry, Alan. You'll be playing near a great side.**"**

BILL SHANKLY

to Alan Ball after he joined Everton

❝I know this is a sad occasion but I think that Dixie would be amazed to know that even in death he could draw a bigger crowd than Everton can on a Saturday afternoon.**❞**

BILL SHANKLY

at Dixie Dean's funeral

❝I'm a people's man.
Only the people matter.**❞**

BILL SHANKLY

"There's Man United and Man City at the bottom of Division One. And by God they'll take some shifting. **"**

BILL SHANKLY

looking at the League table early in the 1972/3 season

"I was the best manager in Britain because I was never devious or cheated anyone. I'd break my wife's legs if I played against her, but I'd never cheat her. **"**

BILL SHANKLY

"Some people believe football is a matter of life and death. I am very disappointed with that attitude. I can assure you it is much more important than that.**"**

BILL SHANKLY

" It wasn't her wedding anniversary, it was her birthday, because there's no way I'd have got married in the football season. And it wasn't Rochdale. It was Rochdale Reserves. **"**

BILL SHANKLY

refuting stories that he had taken his wife Nessie to watch Rochdale on their wedding anniversary

"Some people might think we are lazy, but that's fine. What's the point of tearing players to pieces in the first few days? We never bothered with sand dunes and hills and roads; we trained on grass, where football is played.**"**

BILL SHANKLY

on pre-season training

"Take that poof bandage off, and what do you mean you've hurt your knee? It's Liverpool's knee! **"**

BILL SHANKLY

to an injured Tommy Smith

"Now, boys, Crerand's deceptive, he's slower than you think. **"**

BILL SHANKLY

preparing for a meeting with Paddy Crerand and Manchester United

❝I want to build a team that's invincible, so they'll have to send a team from Mars to beat us. **❞**

BILL SHANKLY

Matt has got a bad back. I tell you it's two bad backs! And not much of a midfield either.

BILL SHANKLY

putting the boot into Matt Busby's Manchester United

“Chairman Mao has never seen such a show of red strength in all his life. **”**

BILL SHANKLY

*addressing 300,000 fans as the 1974 FA Cup
is paraded through the streets of Liverpool*

❝Liverpool was made for me and I was made for Liverpool.**❞**

BILL SHANKLY

CHAPTER 3

RED STARS

"I remember as a new boy looking forward to my first Friday team meeting with some anticipation, so imagine my surprise when Tommy Smith sat down a few chairs away, put his feet up and unfolded his copy of the *Sporting Life*. I was waiting for the sparks to fly but no, Bob just got on with his chat and left Smithy to get on with picking the next day's winners.**"**

PHIL NEAL

"Tommy Smith wasn't born, he was quarried."

DAVID COLEMAN

66 Yes, he misses a few.
But he gets in the right place
to miss them. **99**

BILL SHANKLY

on Roger Hunt

" Keegan had a Doncaster childhood and a Scunthorpe upbringing, yet he seems to have been born with Liverpool in his soul. **"**

JOE MERCER

> **❝**He's just stepped out of the shower. Come in and see him…have a walk round him. He's a colossus. **❞**

BILL SHANKLY

unveiling 6ft 2in, 14-stone centre-half Ron Yeats to journalists

"" Strikers are selfish, at least the very best are. It's not about giving everyone else a chance as far as you are concerned. You want to be out there on the pitch scoring goals. It proves you are a winner. **""**

IAN RUSH

"Who can say what he's going to do? It's a talent and you can't teach it, you can't coach it. All you can do is enjoy it.**"**

ROY EVANS

discussing a young Robbie Fowler

"Robbie Fowler's from the South End of Liverpool, like myself. People from that part of the world need to be tough to survive and make a name for themselves. And believe me, Robbie is tough.**"**

JOHN ALDRIDGE

" No-one has to tell us what we have to do. We play for Liverpool. It is always our intention to win. All the players here want to compete at the top and win. **"**

GEORGINIO WIJNALDUM

the Dutch midfielder states the obvious in September 2018

“ A good skipper, but he could have been a really great one if he had been a bit more extrovert. **”**

BOB PAISLEY

summing up Alan Hansen

"Stevie Nicol, who I played with at Liverpool, was one of the great utility players and now there is another at Anfield in James Milner."**

JAMIE REDKNAPP

"He's a walking advert for the benefits of junk food. He'll eat five packets of crisps and wash it down with Coke and Mars bars.**"**

MARK LAWRENSON

weighs up Steve Nicol's diet

" He was struggling… he was probably too unselfish at the time. That's often the case with a young player, particularly one coming into a successful side. He tended to look for others and lay the ball off when he could have had a go himself. I told him to be a bit more selfish, and it wasn't long before the penny dropped. **"**

BOB PAISLEY

recalling Ian Rush's goal drought when he first arrived at Anfield

❝I'd have to say Steven Gerrard has been the biggest influence on my career so far. I watched him when I was younger and then to go and play and train with him every day was massive for me.**❞**

JORDAN HENDERSON

❝People don't realise that getting married, which Robbie did in the summer, and becoming a family man can affect you. It's a hell of a transition which can have dramatic consequences. I remember Bob Paisley used to say you would have to forget players for up to 12 months if they had just got married and had children.**❞**

IAN RUSH

❝I never saw anyone in this country to touch him. I can think of only two who could go ahead of him – Pele and possibly Cruyff.**❞**

GRAEME SOUNESS

on Kenny Dalglish

"Young Gerrard has the world at his feet. For that age, he's some player, but even now, he could go anywhere, do anything.**"**

BOBBY ROBSON

"Steven Gerrard is Souness
with pace and that's a hell of a player.**"**

ALAN HANSEN

❝I always try to be quick in possession, whether that's running with the ball, playing a quick pass or trying a trick. I really like to dribble with the ball, and that's my role in the team.**❞**

PHILIPPE COUTINHO

"Muhammad Ali, Tiger Woods, Michael Jordan and Diego Maradona. I prefer Pele to Maradona as a player but I'd have Maradona for the laughs.**"**

DANIEL STURRIDGE

reveals his dream dinner companions

" If you ask any of the lads, I think
I can have a laugh just like any
other 20-year-old. But at certain times
I think you've got to be serious and
have your head screwed on. **"**

MICHAEL OWEN

"When you're having a tough time as a team, you all need to stay together. You cannot start becoming individuals.**"**

ADAM LALLANA

“Footballers are recognised everywhere we go. We were in Dublin once, just doing a bit of shopping, and were mobbed in the street. It was like a scene out of a Beatles movie; we had to run to jump into a cab to escape. Another time I was even recognised on the Great Wall of China!**”**

STEVE MCMANAMAN

"You have to accept Luis for what he is. When he played for me at Tenerife, I tried to change him, but you have to say OK, he does what he does and provides different things.**"**

RAFA BENITEZ

on the highly talented but unpredictable Luis Garcia

ff Of course with Phil's skills, everyone wants to give him the ball and wait for something special to happen. Then you think, 'oh no, don't shoot again.' But if I could shoot like he could shoot, then I would try it all the time. **55**

JÜRGEN KLOPP

on Philippe Coutinho

" There's a famous saying in my country, 'O Brasileiro Nao Desiste Nunca,' which means Brazilians never give up. It is a sentence I like and a view I take for life. **"**

PHILIPPE COUTINHO

❝He can pass, he can tackle, he can do almost anything you put to him. The manager at Liverpool keeps telling him he can get better. If he can, he'll be a frightening sight.**❞**

PETER CROUCH

on Steven Gerrard, September 2006

❝Is he the best in the world?
He might not get the attention of
Messi and Ronaldo but yes,
I think he might be. **❞**

ZINEDINE ZIDANE

on Steven Gerrard, March 2009

❝I don't have tattoos, I don't change hairstyles, I don't know how to dance. I just want to play football.**❞**

MOHAMED SALAH

❝What can I say?
I could write a book about his skills,
about his strength, how much I like him,
what a fantastic person he is.
So young, already so mature.**❞**

JÜRGEN KLOPP

gushing praise for Virgil van Dijk as quoted on thisisanfield.com

CHAPTER 4

THE KOP
ON TOP

"Three-one in your Cup final.**"**

Victorious **LIVERPOOL FANS'** *chant to Everton*
following the 3–1 win at Goodison in September 2001

"For those of you watching in black and white, Liverpool are the team with the ball.**"**

LIVERPOOL FANS

joke before the 1984 Milk Cup final with Everton

❝The Kop was the best place in the world to watch football as you were surrounded by so many characters and passionate people. There used to be a bloke called 'the Mad Brickie' who kept us all entertained by getting on the pitch at half-time. **❞**

FAN RICKY TOMLINSON

❝ The Kop's exclusive, an institution, and if you're a member of the Kop you feel you're a member of a society, you've got thousands of friends around you and they're united and loyal. **❞**

BILL SHANKLY

❝That first night was the greatest. We were in the front row of the Kemlyn stand. The whole time my eyes were fixed on the Kop. I couldn't believe it. I was mesmerised. The steam was rising and the noise was incredible.**❞**

PHIL THOMPSON

remembering his first visit to Anfield at the age of 11

" The whole of my life, what they wanted was honesty. They were not so concerned with cultured football, but with triers who gave one hundred per cent. **"**

BOB PAISLEY

on the Kop

❝Tell me ma, me ma,
To put the champagne on ice,
We're going to Cardiff twice,
Tell me ma, me ma.**❞**

LIVERPOOL FANS

to the tune of 'Que Sera' in celebration of their return trip to the
Millennium Stadium for a Cup Final during the historic
Treble season of 2000–01

"When the ball's down the Kop end, they frighten the ball. Sometimes they suck it into the back of the net.**"**

BILL SHANKLY

❝I would just love to have gone and stood in the Kop.❞

KENNY DALGLISH

"You had to be strong to be on the Kop. When I was about 13, I tried to go in the middle where all the excitement was and almost got cut in half. I was only 5ft 7in. A big docker pushed the crowd back and I ducked out and went back to my usual place to the left of the goal.**"**

ELVIS COSTELLO

"There's no noise like the Anfield noise and I love it!**"**

IAN ST JOHN

❝The highlight of the game was not our two goals or the three points we won. It was when our fans made the Kop sing 'You'll Never Walk Alone'. It was as if they couldn't come here and go home without hearing it sung in all its glory. It was very emotional, and something I'll remember forever.**❞**

KEVIN KEEGAN

after Newcastle's 2–0 win at Anfield, 1994

❝I love the scouse soul. I love the way they love life in the city of Liverpool, I love the way they want to be different. They are different. I know a lot of scousers and they are really good people.**❞**

JÜRGEN KLOPP

pays tribute to the good folk of Liverpool

“When we had the lockdown that changed a bit, because I had more time to think. You've got to stay focused, stay positive and pray that you get to finish the season off. It's great to get over the line and finally win the Premier League.**”**

JORDAN HENDERSON

CHAPTER 5

INSIDE THE BOOT ROOM

❝I remember Jimmy Adamson crowing after Burnley had beaten us that his players were in a different league. At the end of the season they were. **❞**

BOB PAISLEY

"Sometimes if you spit up in the air, it can come back in your face.**"**

GERARD HOULLIER

reacting to jibes from Crystal Palace's Clinton Morrison after
the first leg of the 2001 Worthington Cup semi-final

"He was only an ordinary sized man, but he just had this presence, he used to stand so tall. When he stood in front of the Kop he had thousands in the palms of his hands.**"**

FAN RICKY TOMLINSON

in praise of Bill Shankly

"When I left school, the head said,
'I hope you can do something in football
because, if not, I have not the best
feeling for your future.'**"**

JÜRGEN KLOPP

" They say he's tough, he's hard, he's ruthless. Rubbish, he's got a heart of gold, he loves the game, he loves his fans, he loves his players. He's like an old collie dog, he doesn't like hurting his sheep. He'll drive them. Certainly. But bite them, never. **"**

JOE MERCER

on Bill Shankly

" If Bill had one failing, it was the
fact that he did not like to upset
players that had done so well for him.
He was a softie at heart. **"**

BOB PAISLEY

" I am not going to call myself anything. I am a normal guy from the Black Forest. My mother is watching this press conference at home. If you are going to call me anything, call me the 'Normal One'. **"**

JÜRGEN KLOPP

"I love challenges. I like the aggravation that goes with football management.**"**

GRAEME SOUNESS

taking over at Anfield, 1991

"You have to feel a defeat. You cannot say 'I don't care, it's not important.' You always have to strike back. We can say all of these things, but you know you can fall down and then you have to stand up. That's the truth, but it's completely normal – only silly idiots stay on the floor and wait for the next defeat.**"**

JÜRGEN KLOPP

❝I have only felt like this once before, and that was when my father died, because Bill was like a second father to me. **❞**

KEVIN KEEGAN

hearing of Bill Shankly's death

When Bob appeared on television the public saw this guy with the wide grin on his face and that quaint Geordie accent which I could never really understand. He was like everybody's favourite uncle. But there was a completely ruthless streak in Bob. If he decided that a player had to be axed, then that was that. Sentiment did not come into it.

ALAN HANSEN

"I spent the first year on a good horse, but I was like an apprentice riding the Derby favourite. I was cautious and went too wide round the bends. We should have won the Championship.**"**

BOB PAISLEY

"I never wanted the job in the first place.**"**

BOB PAISLEY

“ Bill Shankly set such a high standard. Liverpool have been geared to this sort of thing for 15 years. I have just helped things along. **”**

BOB PAISLEY

on winning his first title

" He's broken that silly myth that nice guys don't win anything. **"**

BRIAN CLOUGH

assessing Bob Paisley's triumphs

> "I'm too old and tired. It's a job for a young man's brains and energy. It's not an eight-hours-a-day-job, it's twenty-four hours a day. And there's no way you can get away from that."

64-year-old **JOE FAGAN**

stepping down as manager

" Our job is to make the fans happy. When we win, 45,000 people go home happy. When we lose, it not only affects them, it affects the cat. **"**

GERARD HOULLIER

❝It's like any relationship. Sometimes it goes wrong and you simply have to work at putting it right again. There's no point trying to pretend it's perfect all the time. We don't sit here holding hands seven days a week.**❞**

ROY EVANS

on his partnership with Gerard Houllier

"Shankly gave the players and the city their pride and passion back. If you didn't have the pride and the passion, then you didn't play for Shankly and you didn't play for Liverpool.**"**

FAN RICKY TOMLINSON

" It's not about the long ball or the short ball, it's about the right ball. **"**

BOB PAISLEY

❝Even Ian Callaghan had to bend down to get through the door after one of Shankly's team talks. It was amazing how he could build you up.**❞**

RON YEATS

" We didn't know what he was talking about half the time but we knew what he wanted. **"**

TOMMY SMITH

trying to follow Bob Paisley's mangled English

" Bob would call us together on a Friday morning and usually just say 'The same team as last week', and we would get on with it. **"**

MARK LAWRENSON

"What do I say to them in the dressing-room? Nothing really. Most of the time I don't even know what they are going to do myself. **"**

KENNY DALGLISH

" Just a thought! Woke up with Liverpool manager lying beside me! Twenty years since that happened! **"**

MARINA DALGLISH

tweets her excitement

" You know I could have stayed in my comfortable chair in South Wales having the first Welsh team that got promoted and been there a number of years, but for me I wanted to work at a club that was world class and at the very, very top. **"**

BRENDAN RODGERS

**"The fans deserve to know the truth –
Firmino copies me,
not me copying him!"**

SADIO MANE

tries to rebuff suggestions he copied his team-mates' goal celebrations

❝Our ambition is to increase the capacity of Anfield stadium and allow more fans to enjoy some of the best football in the world.❞

ANDY HUGHES

Liverpool's chief operating officer commenting on the expansion plans for the Anfield Road stand in November 2019

❝I don't think it's possible but because it's you, I think we have a chance.**❞**

JÜRGEN KLOPP

team talk before the second leg of their 2019 Champions League semi-final game against Barcelona, trailing 3-0 from the first leg

❝Without this manager this is impossible...
What he has done since coming in is
unbelievable... There's such togetherness,
he has created a special dressing room...
I'm so proud to be a part of this football club
and to cap it with this is so special
to me. **❞**

JORDAN HENDERSON

The Liverpool captain after lifting the Champions League trophy in 2019

"I've had good parts in my career but not this good. It is difficult to get here and it is all about the boys' commitment, desire and understanding of the club's heart and soul. The consistency the boys have showed is exceptional. We will not stop.**"**

JÜRGEN KLOPP

after securing a first Premier League title in 30 years

" The club has grown and this squad is capable of going on and doing this again, it really is. Fair play to Klopp, he could have had the pick of any club potentially, but he came in and said we can win the league in five years and rewrite our own history. **"**

ROBBIE FOWLER

confirmed Jurgen Klopp fan

CHAPTER 6

COMINGS AND GOINGS

❝When I went to see the chairman to tell him, it was like walking to the electric chair.**❞**

BILL SHANKLY

on his decision to quit

❝I had to say I was retiring, though I believe you retire when you're in a coffin and the lid is nailed down and your name is on it. **❞**

BILL SHANKLY

" Don't you recognise him? This man is the future captain of England. **"**

BILL SHANKLY

*to a traffic policeman who had stopped him on his way back
to Liverpool with new signing, Emlyn Hughes*

" Kenny Dalglish was the reason I signed for Liverpool. It was his reputation and his stature in the game that persuaded me and the fact that he gave me a particularly smart pair of boots. It is the only 'bung' I have ever received. They were two sizes too big for me, but I didn't half look good in them. **"**

STEVE MCMANAMAN

"Playing Roma in Rome in the European Cup final and scoring a penalty in the shoot-out to help us win it. That was my very last kick for Liverpool and it doesn't really get any better than that. **"**

GRAEME SOUNESS

"I know that Jamie Carragher is a legend here in Liverpool and hopefully I will be as well. I want to be a legend one day. That's why I try always to give my best.**"**

EMRE CAN

"He is the best player that
Liverpool have signed this century.
It was the best decision we have ever made.
He sets such a fine example, not just to our
players but to everybody in the game. **"**

Chairman **JOHN SMITH**
praising Kenny Dalglish as Liverpool clinch the League title in 1986

" Management is a seven-days-a-week job. The intensity of it takes its toll on your health. Some people want to go on for ever, and I obviously don't. **"**

KENNY DALGLISH

1991

❝The chief executive, Peter Robinson, and I had just sat down at our fortnightly meeting with the manager when he came out and said he wanted to finish. I jokingly said: 'This afternoon?' and he said: 'Yes'. **❞**

Liverpool chairman **NOEL WHITE**
reeling from Kenny Dalglish's shock departure

"I have always wanted to come
back and it has been a long time
but I'm glad to say I'm back now. Leaving
was probably one of my biggest regrets I
have had in football. I'm chuffed to bits.
I can't really believe it's happened again
so I'm ecstatic.**"**

Kop favourite **ROBBIE FOWLER**
rejoins Liverpool, January 2006

133

❝I'm delighted that he has signed.
I think he's one of the top strikers
in world football.**❞**

BRENDAN RODGERS

*on Luis Suarez, after the Uruguayan entered into a new long-term
contract following the London 2012 Olympic Games football tournament*

"He is a perfectionist and so everyone wants to be like him. You want to give perfection during training and give 100 per cent on the pitch. It is great to see how intense he is on the touchline. He is really emotional and shows that in every part of the game. **"**

DEJAN LOVREN

on Jurgen Klopp

❝I can never thank you enough for what you have given me during this time and no matter where I go in the world, for the rest of my life, I will always cherish Liverpool in my heart. You, the club and the city will always be a part of me.**❞**

PHILIPPE COUTINHO

thanks the Liverpool supporters after his £142 million transfer to Barcelona in January 2018

❝With experience, the nervousness is not there. When I made my debut for Liverpool against Everton, I was more excited than nervous. I surprised myself that day with my calm. **❞**

VIRGIL VAN DIJK

didn't feel the pressure of being the world's most expensive defender in January 2018

CHAPTER 7

SECRETS
OF SUCCESS

❝Tommy Smith would start a riot in a graveyard.**❞**

BILL SHANKLY

"When you see Tommy Smith go down, then you know he's been hurt.**"**

BOB PAISLEY

❝We do things together. I'd walk into the toughest dockside pub in the world with this lot because you know that if things got tough, nobody would 'bottle' it and scoot off.**❞**

EMLYN HUGHES

on his Liverpool team-mates

" If I told people that the secret of Liverpool's success is a dip in the Mersey three times a week, I not only reckon they'd believe me but I think our river would be full of footballers from all over the country. **"**

Club trainer **RONNIE MORAN**

" There's so many clubs been ruined by people's ego. The day after we won our first European Cup, we were back at this club at 9.45 in the morning, talking about how we would do it again, working from that moment, because nobody has the right to win anything they haven't earned. **"**

BOB PAISLEY

" Bottle is a quality too, you know. It's not just about ball control and being clever. Sometimes you have to show the world what's between your legs. **"**

GRAEME SOUNESS

"I love tackling. It's better than sex. A great tackle gets everybody pumped up. **"**

PAUL INCE

" To be the best you have to forget the partying and concentrate all your energies on the football. **"**

MICHAEL OWEN

" Liverpool players must play like a lion, give his all. There must be determination, commitment and resolve to be a Liverpool player. **"**

GERARD HOULLIER

"How did they do it? Liverpool had belief, hunger, desire, attitude and had a crowd that was willing them on from the very first second. Liverpool showed their intent right from the off.**"**

ALAN SHEARER

praises Liverpool after the 2019 Champions League semi-final

MAGIC MOMENTS

❝We wore the all red strip for the first time.
Christ, the players looked like giants. And we
played like giants. **❞**

BILL SHANKLY

*after Liverpool had worn their all-red kit for the first time, against
Anderlecht at Anfield, 25 November 1964*

"Getting the Nou Camp booing their own players because they didn't touch the ball in the first ten minutes. **"**

EMLYN HUGHES
recalling his favourite moment from Liverpool's triumphant 1976
UEFA Cup run – a semi-final trip to Barcelona

"This is the greatest night in Liverpool's history. This is the result of planning, of simplicity, of how to play the game in a simple manner. I think the whole world realises that it's the way to play.**"**

BILL SHANKLY

after watching the 1977 European Cup final

❝I was really confident. I took a penalty in training and put it in the same spot. Just like that. **❞**

ALAN KENNEDY

after scoring the winning penalty in the
European Cup Final shoot-out against Roma in 1984

❝As the ball came over, I remembered what Graham Taylor said about my having no right foot, so I headed it in.**❞**

JOHN BARNES
scoring against Taylor's Aston Villa in a 1988 FA Cup tie

❝When you play in a European final, you are looking for immortality. People remember who was playing and when you look at programmes from finals you just recall the facts of the game. These boys have produced a game which will be remembered for a long time. **❞**

GERARD HOULLIER

after the 2001 UEFA Cup final

“For far too long our fans have had to see a team in the backwaters of English football, so it is great to have people talking about Liverpool again.**”**

PHIL THOMPSON

celebrating the 2001 treble

❝I think the game will be
a dull 0–0. **❞**

JORDI CRUYFF

of Alaves before the UEFA Cup Final
which Liverpool won 5–4, May 2001

❝I thought it was a bit cruel of Liverpool to put Steven Gerrard on when we were getting tired!**❞**

Total Network Solutions boss **KEN McKENNA** *after his club's 3–0 defeat at Anfield in the qualifying round of the Champions League, July 2005*

❝I just wanted to jump into the stand and start celebrating with those wonderful fans.**❞**

STEVEN GERRARD

on overcoming Chelsea in the 2005 Champions League semi-final

❝Liverpool produced one of the greatest comebacks in the history of football. They created for themselves an utter disaster and somehow turned a lost match around in six impossible minutes… The tide turned in a manner that defied logical and even tactical sense. It was simply as if God had changed sides.**❞**

SIMON BARNES

in The Times on the 2005 Champions League Final

> **"** Amazing, astounding, awe-inspiring, breathtaking, extraordinary, hair-raising, heart-stirring, magnificent, marvellous, miraculous, moving, overwhelming, spectacular, spine-tingling, striking, stunning, stupefying, stupendous, wonderful. **"**

LIVERPOOL FC'S OFFICIAL WEBSITE

on the Reds' great fightback

" Carra came up to me like he was crazy. He grabbed me and said, 'Jerzy, Jerzy, Jerzy – remember Bruce [Grobbelaar]? He did crazy things in 1984. You have to do the same.' He told me I would be the hero. **"**

JERZY DUDEK

on what he called his 'starfish with jelly legs' routine during the Champions League Final penalty shoot-out

❝We talked at half-time and told the players that we needed to believe. We started to press with more energy and the belief came back. I was so proud of my players in extra-time – this was the greatest night I've had as a manager.**❞**

RAFA BENITEZ

" I'm on top of the world.
This is the best night of my life. **"**

STEVEN GERRARD

after holding aloft the European Cup, May 2005

"I've watched in my life so many football games, I can't remember a lot like this. You play against maybe the best team in the world, you're not allowed to concede, you have to score... Winning is already difficult, but winning with a clean sheet? I don't know how we did it.**"**

JÜRGEN KLOPP

being interviewed after the dramatic 4-0 win over Barcelona in the
2019 Champions League semi-final second leg

" Steven Gerrard could play right-back and still be effective because these are world-class players. I wish he had been at right-back though! **"**

Burnley boss **OWEN COYLE**
after seeing his side hammered by Liverpool, September 2009

❝I don't know when the last time we were there was, but we know where we are going. We've maybe forgotten the route because we've not been there for a while, but I'm sure the driver will remember. **❞**

KENNY DALGLISH

relishing Liverpool's first trip to Wembley since 1996

❝I kicked every ball tonight. I'm more tired now than when I play!**❞**

Injured **STEVEN GERRARD**
after watching the 4–4 draw with Arsenal in a TV studio, April 2009

"I think anyone who has ever won a trophy, whether it's at Wembley or wherever, has come away and said, 'I enjoyed that, I'd love to do it again'.**"**

KENNY DALGLISH

after Liverpool had won the Carling Cup, 2012

"I am so happy for the boys, all these people, and my family. They suffer for me, they deserve it more than anybody. Did you ever see a team like this, fighting with no fuel in the tank? It is the best night of our professional lives.**"**

JÜRGEN KLOPP

enjoys the moment after the Reds won the 2019 Champions League

❝I am just a normal lad from Liverpool whose dream has just come true. **❞**

TRENT ALEXANDER-ARNOLD

celebrates that night in Madrid, 2019

❝Last year we finished second
with 97 points and we knew we were on the
periphery of something great.**❞**

ROBBIE FOWLER

"I called my family 10 seconds before the final whistle. We had a Facetime call. I told them I loved them, they told me they loved me. All the other messages, maybe I should use this opportunity to say sorry I cannot answer all of them, but I will read all of them. **"**

JÜRGEN KLOPP

reveals who his first port of call was when celebrating the title

" Sorry, I can't concentrate on the interview because a load of Facetime Contact Requests keep popping up on the interview screen. Bwip! Bwip! Bwip! **"**

JORDAN HENDERSON

interviewed shortly after Liverpool clinched the title

" Unbelievable. What a season so far.
Incredible, incredible, to be part of this group
of players. I'm very proud to call myself a
Premier League winner... We're all proud
of each other, I can't really describe
the feeling. **"**

VIRGIL VAN DIJK

attempts to express his happiness

177

"What is more important – is it talent, is it attitude? I think the easy answer is that without talent you are nothing... Everybody saw what a great player you are, everybody saw what a great personality you are, what a great character you are... Enjoy the moment, and, again: best player of the Premier League. Wow!**"**

JÜRGEN KLOPP

*in a special video message to Jordan Henderson, winner of the
2020 Football Writers' Association Player of the Year award*

"This was a season for the ages and for the faithful of Liverpool Football Club. It has been an incredible year of magnificent achievement culminating tonight in capturing the Premier League title.**"**

Owner **JOHN W. HENRY**
via Twitter

CHAPTER 9

YOU'LL NEVER WALK ALONE

❝I've been on this planet
for 45 years, and have supported
Liverpool for 42 of them. **❞**

ROY EVANS

becoming manager in 1994

66 He was the same as me,
a Liverpool fan from a council estate who
loved his footy and kicked a ball around
in the street. **99**

STEVEN GERRARD

remembering his cousin, Jon-Paul Gilhooley,
who died in the Hillsborough tragedy, aged 10

❝ The fans were the innocent victims of a tragedy caused by the criminal neglect of the people you believed were there to protect you. But for 23 years the fans were portrayed as responsible for the disaster, effectively branded murderers. **❞**

ROBBIE FOWLER

reacts to the Hillsborough Independent Panel's report

"To an awful lot of people,
now you understand why we couldn't
just get over it. **"**

PHIL THOMPSON

on Twitter

"If we had to lose our record, I'd sooner it be against Liverpool than anyone else.**"**

Newcastle boss **KEVIN KEEGAN** *as Liverpool became the first team that season to take a point at St James' Park, 1994*

186

❝Worldwide, Liverpool's a club that is renowned throughout. I think you go to wherever, Kuala Lumpur, New Zealand, as far away as you can, everyone knows about Liverpool.**❞**

BRENDAN RODGERS

just before his first Merseyside derby, 2012

❝Think my chances of making the Liverpool side are gone now. Might still be able to get a game at one of those London clubs though. **❞**

Liverpool fan **JOHN PEEL**

at his 50th birthday party

❝I love the club, the fans and the city and, with a club like this and supporters like this, I could never say no to staying.❞

RAFA BENITEZ

committing himself to Liverpool until 2014

❝LFC has made the beautiful game
more beautiful than ever. **❞**

Owner **JOHN W. HENRY**
via Twitter

❝It's so special to be a part of this football team. **❞**

JORDAN HENDERSON

❝Walk on, walk on,
With hope in your heart,
And you'll never walk alone,
You'll never walk alone.**❞**

THE KOP CHOIR

every home game from 1963 to the present day